50 Delicious Premium Steak Recipes

By: Kelly Johnson

Table of Contents

- Classic Ribeye Steak
- Filet Mignon with Garlic Herb Butter
- New York Strip with Peppercorn Sauce
- T-Bone Steak with Chimichurri
- Porterhouse Steak with Garlic Butter
- Skirt Steak with Salsa Verde
- Flank Steak with Balsamic Glaze
- Sirloin Steak with Red Wine Reduction
- Tomahawk Steak with Rosemary Butter
- Bavette Steak with Shallot Sauce
- Wagyu Steak with Truffle Salt
- Coffee-Rubbed Steak
- Grilled Steak with Blue Cheese Crumbles
- Steak Diane
- Teriyaki Steak
- Cajun-Spiced Steak
- Garlic-Parmesan Crusted Steak
- Steak au Poivre
- Korean BBQ Bulgogi Steak
- Chimichurri-Marinated Skirt Steak
- Grilled Hanger Steak with Herb Butter
- Rosemary and Thyme Strip Steak
- Smoked Tri-Tip Steak
- Cuban Mojo Marinated Steak
- Blackened Ribeye
- Bourbon-Glazed Sirloin
- Pan-Seared Tenderloin Medallions
- Steak Tacos with Lime Crema
- Honey Garlic Flank Steak
- Gorgonzola-Stuffed Filet
- Argentinean Grilled Steak
- Sesame-Ginger Marinated Steak
- Red Chimichurri Picanha
- Grilled Steak Salad with Mustard Vinaigrette
- Chipotle Lime Flank Steak

- Steak Fajitas
- Balsamic Rosemary Hanger Steak
- Char-Grilled Porterhouse with Compound Butter
- Steak and Mushroom Sauce
- Citrus-Marinated Tri-Tip
- Garlic Butter Steak Bites
- Steak Skewers with Peanut Sauce
- Cajun Steak Alfredo
- Spicy Thai Basil Beef
- Steak and Shrimp Surf & Turf
- Maple Glazed Steak Tips
- Sous Vide Filet Mignon
- Grilled Steak with Blackberry Sauce
- Herb-Crusted Prime Ribeye
- Braised Short Ribs with Red Wine Reduction

Classic Ribeye Steak

Ingredients:

- 2 ribeye steaks (1–1.5 inches thick)
- 2 tablespoons olive oil
- Salt and freshly ground black pepper, to taste
- 2 cloves garlic, smashed
- 2 sprigs fresh thyme
- 2 tablespoons unsalted butter

Instructions:

1. **Prepare steaks:** Pat steaks dry, rub with olive oil, and season with salt and pepper.
2. **Cook:** Heat a skillet over high heat, sear steaks for 3–4 minutes per side. Add garlic, thyme, and butter, basting during the last minute.
3. **Rest:** Remove from heat, rest for 5 minutes before serving.

Filet Mignon with Garlic Herb Butter

Ingredients:

- 2 filet mignon steaks
- Salt and freshly ground black pepper, to taste
- 2 tablespoons olive oil
- 1/4 cup unsalted butter, softened
- 1 clove garlic, minced
- 1 teaspoon fresh parsley, minced

Instructions:

1. **Prepare butter:** Mix butter, garlic, and parsley; set aside.
2. **Cook steaks:** Season steaks and sear in olive oil for 3–4 minutes per side over medium-high heat. Finish in the oven at 400°F (200°C) for 5–7 minutes.
3. **Serve:** Top each steak with garlic herb butter before serving.

New York Strip with Peppercorn Sauce

Ingredients:

- 2 New York strip steaks
- Salt and freshly ground black pepper, to taste
- 2 tablespoons olive oil
- 1/4 cup green peppercorns
- 1/2 cup heavy cream
- 1/4 cup beef stock

Instructions:

1. **Cook steaks:** Season and sear steaks in olive oil for 4 minutes per side. Remove and let rest.
2. **Make sauce:** Add peppercorns to the pan, followed by cream and stock. Simmer until thickened.
3. **Serve:** Spoon sauce over steaks.

T-Bone Steak with Chimichurri

Ingredients:

- 2 T-bone steaks
- Salt and freshly ground black pepper, to taste
- 2 tablespoons olive oil
- 1 cup fresh parsley, chopped
- 1/2 cup olive oil
- 2 tablespoons red wine vinegar
- 1 clove garlic, minced
- 1 teaspoon crushed red pepper

Instructions:

1. **Prepare chimichurri:** Mix parsley, olive oil, vinegar, garlic, and red pepper; season to taste.
2. **Cook steaks:** Season steaks, sear in olive oil for 4–5 minutes per side. Rest for 5 minutes.
3. **Serve:** Top steaks with chimichurri sauce.

Porterhouse Steak with Garlic Butter

Ingredients:

- 2 porterhouse steaks
- Salt and freshly ground black pepper, to taste
- 2 tablespoons olive oil
- 2 tablespoons unsalted butter
- 2 cloves garlic, minced

Instructions:

1. **Cook steaks:** Season steaks, sear in olive oil for 4–5 minutes per side.
2. **Add butter:** Add butter and garlic to the pan, baste steaks for 1–2 minutes.
3. **Rest:** Let steaks rest for 5 minutes before serving.

Skirt Steak with Salsa Verde

Ingredients:

- 1 1/2 lbs skirt steak
- Salt and freshly ground black pepper, to taste
- 1/4 cup olive oil
- 1/2 cup fresh parsley
- 1/4 cup fresh cilantro
- 1 clove garlic, minced
- Juice of 1 lemon

Instructions:

1. **Make salsa verde:** Blend parsley, cilantro, garlic, lemon juice, and olive oil; season to taste.
2. **Cook steak:** Season steak, sear on high heat for 2–3 minutes per side. Rest for 5 minutes.
3. **Serve:** Slice steak and drizzle with salsa verde.

Flank Steak with Balsamic Glaze

Ingredients:

- 1 1/2 lbs flank steak
- Salt and freshly ground black pepper, to taste
- 2 tablespoons olive oil
- 1/4 cup balsamic vinegar
- 2 tablespoons brown sugar

Instructions:

1. **Prepare glaze:** Simmer balsamic vinegar and brown sugar until reduced.
2. **Cook steak:** Season steak, sear in olive oil for 4–5 minutes per side. Rest for 5 minutes.
3. **Serve:** Drizzle steak with balsamic glaze before slicing.

Sirloin Steak with Red Wine Reduction

Ingredients:

- 2 sirloin steaks
- Salt and freshly ground black pepper, to taste
- 2 tablespoons olive oil
- 1/2 cup red wine
- 1/4 cup beef stock
- 1 tablespoon butter

Instructions:

1. **Cook steaks:** Season and sear steaks in olive oil for 4 minutes per side. Remove and let rest.
2. **Make reduction:** Add wine and stock to the pan, simmer until reduced. Stir in butter.
3. **Serve:** Pour sauce over steaks.

Tomahawk Steak with Rosemary Butter

Ingredients:

- 1 tomahawk steak
- Salt and freshly ground black pepper, to taste
- 2 tablespoons olive oil
- 2 tablespoons unsalted butter
- 1 sprig fresh rosemary

Instructions:

1. **Cook steak:** Season steak, sear on high heat for 4–5 minutes per side. Finish in a 375°F (190°C) oven for 10–15 minutes.
2. **Add butter:** Melt butter with rosemary, basting steak during cooking.
3. **Rest:** Let steak rest for 10 minutes before serving.

Bavette Steak with Shallot Sauce

Ingredients:

- 1 1/2 lbs bavette steak
- Salt and freshly ground black pepper, to taste
- 2 tablespoons olive oil
- 2 shallots, minced
- 1/2 cup beef stock
- 1/4 cup red wine
- 1 tablespoon butter

Instructions:

1. **Cook steak:** Season steak, sear in olive oil for 4 minutes per side. Remove and let rest.
2. **Make sauce:** Sauté shallots, deglaze with wine, and add stock. Simmer until reduced, then stir in butter.
3. **Serve:** Pour sauce over sliced steak.

Wagyu Steak with Truffle Salt

Ingredients:

- 2 Wagyu steaks
- Salt and freshly ground black pepper, to taste
- 1 tablespoon olive oil
- 1 teaspoon truffle salt
- 1 tablespoon unsalted butter
- 2 sprigs fresh thyme

Instructions:

1. **Season steaks:** Season Wagyu steaks with salt and pepper.
2. **Cook steaks:** Heat olive oil in a skillet over medium-high heat. Sear steaks for 2–3 minutes per side. Add butter and thyme during the last minute, basting the steaks.
3. **Serve:** Sprinkle truffle salt over the steaks before serving.

Coffee-Rubbed Steak

Ingredients:

- 2 steaks (ribeye, flank, or sirloin)
- 2 tablespoons ground coffee
- 1 tablespoon brown sugar
- 1 teaspoon smoked paprika
- 1/2 teaspoon garlic powder
- Salt and freshly ground black pepper, to taste

Instructions:

1. **Prepare rub:** Combine ground coffee, brown sugar, paprika, garlic powder, salt, and pepper in a small bowl.
2. **Season steaks:** Coat the steaks generously with the coffee rub.
3. **Cook steaks:** Sear steaks in a hot skillet for 3–4 minutes per side, adjusting the heat as needed. Rest before serving.

Grilled Steak with Blue Cheese Crumbles

Ingredients:

- 2 steaks (New York strip or ribeye)
- Salt and freshly ground black pepper, to taste
- 1/4 cup blue cheese crumbles
- 2 tablespoons olive oil
- Fresh herbs (rosemary or thyme) for garnish

Instructions:

1. **Season steaks:** Rub steaks with olive oil and season with salt and pepper.
2. **Grill steaks:** Preheat grill to medium-high heat. Grill steaks for 4–5 minutes per side for medium-rare.
3. **Top with cheese:** Remove from grill, top with blue cheese crumbles, and let rest for 5 minutes before serving. Garnish with fresh herbs.

Steak Diane

Ingredients:

- 2 filet mignon or sirloin steaks
- Salt and freshly ground black pepper, to taste
- 2 tablespoons olive oil
- 1/4 cup brandy
- 1/2 cup heavy cream
- 1 tablespoon Dijon mustard
- 2 tablespoons unsalted butter
- 1/4 cup finely chopped shallots
- 1/4 cup beef stock

Instructions:

1. **Cook steaks:** Season steaks and sear in olive oil for 3–4 minutes per side. Remove and set aside.
2. **Make sauce:** In the same pan, sauté shallots, deglaze with brandy, and stir in mustard, cream, and beef stock. Simmer until thickened.
3. **Finish:** Stir in butter, then return steaks to the pan to coat with the sauce. Serve immediately.

Teriyaki Steak

Ingredients:

- 2 flank steaks
- 1/4 cup soy sauce
- 2 tablespoons honey
- 2 tablespoons rice vinegar
- 1 tablespoon sesame oil
- 2 cloves garlic, minced
- 1 tablespoon fresh ginger, grated

Instructions:

1. **Marinate steaks:** Combine soy sauce, honey, rice vinegar, sesame oil, garlic, and ginger in a bowl. Marinate steaks for at least 30 minutes.
2. **Cook steaks:** Preheat grill to medium-high heat. Grill steaks for 3–4 minutes per side for medium.
3. **Serve:** Slice thinly against the grain and drizzle with any remaining marinade.

Cajun-Spiced Steak

Ingredients:

- 2 steaks (ribeye or sirloin)
- 1 tablespoon paprika
- 1 teaspoon cayenne pepper
- 1 teaspoon garlic powder
- 1 teaspoon onion powder
- Salt and freshly ground black pepper, to taste
- 2 tablespoons olive oil

Instructions:

1. **Prepare rub:** Combine paprika, cayenne, garlic powder, onion powder, salt, and pepper in a bowl.
2. **Season steaks:** Coat steaks evenly with the spice rub.
3. **Cook steaks:** Heat olive oil in a skillet over medium-high heat and cook steaks for 4–5 minutes per side. Rest before serving.

Garlic-Parmesan Crusted Steak

Ingredients:

- 2 steaks (New York strip or ribeye)
- Salt and freshly ground black pepper, to taste
- 2 tablespoons olive oil
- 1/4 cup grated Parmesan cheese
- 2 cloves garlic, minced
- 1 tablespoon chopped fresh parsley

Instructions:

1. **Season steaks:** Season steaks with salt and pepper.
2. **Cook steaks:** Heat olive oil in a skillet over medium-high heat. Sear steaks for 3–4 minutes per side.
3. **Top with Parmesan:** In the last minute of cooking, top each steak with garlic and Parmesan. Cover briefly to melt the cheese. Serve with chopped parsley.

Steak au Poivre

Ingredients:

- 2 filet mignon steaks
- 1 tablespoon black peppercorns, crushed
- Salt, to taste
- 2 tablespoons olive oil
- 1/2 cup cognac or brandy
- 1/2 cup heavy cream
- 2 tablespoons unsalted butter

Instructions:

1. **Prepare steaks:** Press crushed peppercorns onto both sides of the steaks. Season with salt.
2. **Cook steaks:** Heat olive oil in a skillet and sear steaks for 3–4 minutes per side. Remove steaks from the pan.
3. **Make sauce:** Add cognac to the pan, deglaze, and reduce. Stir in cream and butter, then return steaks to the pan, basting with the sauce. Serve immediately.

Korean BBQ Bulgogi Steak

Ingredients:

- 1 lb skirt steak, thinly sliced
- 1/4 cup soy sauce
- 2 tablespoons brown sugar
- 1 tablespoon sesame oil
- 2 cloves garlic, minced
- 1 tablespoon fresh ginger, grated
- 2 tablespoons rice vinegar
- 2 tablespoons gochujang (Korean chili paste)
- 2 tablespoons toasted sesame seeds

Instructions:

1. **Marinate steak:** Mix soy sauce, brown sugar, sesame oil, garlic, ginger, rice vinegar, and gochujang in a bowl. Marinate steak for at least 30 minutes.
2. **Cook steak:** Heat a skillet over medium-high heat. Cook the steak for 2–3 minutes per side, until browned and cooked through.
3. **Serve:** Sprinkle with toasted sesame seeds and serve with rice and vegetables.

Chimichurri-Marinated Skirt Steak

Ingredients:

- 2 skirt steaks
- 1/4 cup olive oil
- 1/4 cup red wine vinegar
- 2 tablespoons fresh parsley, chopped
- 2 tablespoons fresh cilantro, chopped
- 2 garlic cloves, minced
- 1 teaspoon red pepper flakes
- Salt and freshly ground black pepper, to taste

Instructions:

1. **Make chimichurri marinade:** Combine olive oil, red wine vinegar, parsley, cilantro, garlic, red pepper flakes, salt, and pepper in a bowl.
2. **Marinate steak:** Coat the skirt steaks with the chimichurri marinade and refrigerate for at least 1 hour.
3. **Cook steaks:** Preheat grill to medium-high heat. Grill the steaks for 3–4 minutes per side. Serve with extra chimichurri sauce on top.

Grilled Hanger Steak with Herb Butter

Ingredients:

- 2 hanger steaks
- Salt and freshly ground black pepper, to taste
- 2 tablespoons olive oil
- 1/4 cup unsalted butter, softened
- 2 tablespoons fresh rosemary, chopped
- 1 tablespoon fresh thyme, chopped
- 1 clove garlic, minced

Instructions:

1. **Season steaks:** Rub the hanger steaks with olive oil, salt, and pepper.
2. **Grill steaks:** Preheat grill to medium-high heat and grill steaks for 4–5 minutes per side for medium-rare.
3. **Make herb butter:** In a small bowl, mix softened butter, rosemary, thyme, and garlic.
4. **Serve:** Top grilled steaks with herb butter and allow it to melt before serving.

Rosemary and Thyme Strip Steak

Ingredients:

- 2 New York strip steaks
- 1 tablespoon fresh rosemary, chopped
- 1 tablespoon fresh thyme, chopped
- Salt and freshly ground black pepper, to taste
- 2 tablespoons olive oil
- 2 cloves garlic, minced

Instructions:

1. **Season steaks:** Mix rosemary, thyme, salt, and pepper. Rub the mixture into both sides of the steaks.
2. **Cook steaks:** Heat olive oil in a skillet over medium-high heat. Add garlic and sear the steaks for 4–5 minutes per side for medium-rare.
3. **Rest and serve:** Let steaks rest for 5 minutes, then serve.

Smoked Tri-Tip Steak

Ingredients:

- 1 tri-tip steak
- 1 tablespoon olive oil
- 2 teaspoons smoked paprika
- 1 teaspoon garlic powder
- 1 teaspoon onion powder
- 1/2 teaspoon cayenne pepper
- Salt and freshly ground black pepper, to taste

Instructions:

1. **Prepare steak:** Rub tri-tip with olive oil, paprika, garlic powder, onion powder, cayenne, salt, and pepper.
2. **Smoke steak:** Preheat smoker to 225°F. Smoke the tri-tip for 2–3 hours until it reaches an internal temperature of 135°F for medium-rare.
3. **Finish and serve:** Rest for 10 minutes before slicing and serving.

Cuban Mojo Marinated Steak

Ingredients:

- 2 flank steaks
- 1/4 cup orange juice
- 1/4 cup lime juice
- 1/4 cup olive oil
- 3 cloves garlic, minced
- 1 tablespoon fresh cilantro, chopped
- 1 teaspoon ground cumin
- 1/2 teaspoon ground oregano
- Salt and freshly ground black pepper, to taste

Instructions:

1. **Make marinade:** Combine orange juice, lime juice, olive oil, garlic, cilantro, cumin, oregano, salt, and pepper.
2. **Marinate steak:** Coat steaks with the marinade and refrigerate for at least 1 hour.
3. **Cook steak:** Preheat grill to medium-high heat. Grill steaks for 4–5 minutes per side, then slice and serve with extra cilantro.

Blackened Ribeye

Ingredients:

- 2 ribeye steaks
- 1 tablespoon paprika
- 1 teaspoon garlic powder
- 1 teaspoon onion powder
- 1/2 teaspoon cayenne pepper
- 1/2 teaspoon dried thyme
- Salt and freshly ground black pepper, to taste
- 2 tablespoons butter

Instructions:

1. **Prepare seasoning:** Mix paprika, garlic powder, onion powder, cayenne, thyme, salt, and pepper in a bowl.
2. **Season steaks:** Coat ribeye steaks with the seasoning blend.
3. **Cook steaks:** Heat butter in a skillet over high heat. Sear steaks for 4–5 minutes per side until a crust forms. Serve immediately.

Bourbon-Glazed Sirloin

Ingredients:

- 2 sirloin steaks
- Salt and freshly ground black pepper, to taste
- 1/4 cup bourbon
- 2 tablespoons brown sugar
- 2 tablespoons soy sauce
- 1 tablespoon Dijon mustard
- 1/4 teaspoon ground black pepper

Instructions:

1. **Season steaks:** Season sirloin steaks with salt and pepper.
2. **Cook steaks:** Sear steaks in a hot skillet for 4–5 minutes per side for medium.
3. **Make bourbon glaze:** In the same skillet, add bourbon, brown sugar, soy sauce, mustard, and black pepper. Simmer until the glaze thickens, about 3 minutes.
4. **Finish:** Brush the glaze over the steaks before serving.

Pan-Seared Tenderloin Medallions

Ingredients:

- 2 tenderloin medallions
- Salt and freshly ground black pepper, to taste
- 2 tablespoons olive oil
- 1/4 cup red wine
- 1/4 cup beef broth
- 2 tablespoons unsalted butter

Instructions:

1. **Season steaks:** Season medallions with salt and pepper.
2. **Cook steaks:** Heat olive oil in a skillet over medium-high heat. Sear medallions for 3–4 minutes per side.
3. **Make sauce:** Add wine and beef broth to the pan. Simmer until reduced by half, then stir in butter.
4. **Serve:** Drizzle sauce over medallions before serving.

Steak Tacos with Lime Crema

Ingredients:

- 2 skirt steaks
- Salt and freshly ground black pepper, to taste
- 8 small tortillas
- 1 cup shredded lettuce
- 1/2 cup diced tomatoes
- 1/4 cup shredded cheese
- 1/4 cup sour cream
- 1 tablespoon lime juice
- 1 tablespoon fresh cilantro, chopped

Instructions:

1. **Cook steaks:** Season skirt steaks with salt and pepper. Grill for 3–4 minutes per side. Slice thinly.
2. **Make lime crema:** Mix sour cream, lime juice, and cilantro.
3. **Assemble tacos:** Warm tortillas and top with steak, lettuce, tomatoes, cheese, and a drizzle of lime crema. Serve immediately.

Honey Garlic Flank Steak

Ingredients:

- 2 flank steaks
- 1/4 cup honey
- 1/4 cup soy sauce
- 3 cloves garlic, minced
- 1 tablespoon apple cider vinegar
- 1 teaspoon ginger, grated

Instructions:

1. **Make marinade:** Combine honey, soy sauce, garlic, vinegar, and ginger in a bowl.
2. **Marinate steak:** Coat the flank steaks with marinade and refrigerate for at least 2 hours.
3. **Cook steak:** Preheat grill to medium-high heat. Grill the steaks for 4–5 minutes per side. Slice against the grain and serve.

Gorgonzola-Stuffed Filet

Ingredients:

- 2 filet mignon steaks
- 1/4 cup crumbled Gorgonzola cheese
- 2 tablespoons cream cheese, softened
- 1 tablespoon fresh thyme, chopped
- Salt and freshly ground black pepper, to taste
- 2 tablespoons olive oil

Instructions:

1. **Prepare stuffing:** Mix Gorgonzola cheese, cream cheese, and fresh thyme in a small bowl.
2. **Stuff the filets:** Cut a small slit into the side of each filet to create a pocket. Stuff with the Gorgonzola mixture.
3. **Cook steaks:** Heat olive oil in a skillet over medium-high heat. Sear filets for 4-5 minutes per side for medium-rare.
4. **Serve:** Let steaks rest for 5 minutes before serving.

Argentinean Grilled Steak

Ingredients:

- 2 ribeye steaks
- 2 tablespoons olive oil
- 2 cloves garlic, minced
- 2 tablespoons fresh parsley, chopped
- 1 tablespoon lemon juice
- 1 teaspoon smoked paprika
- Salt and freshly ground black pepper, to taste

Instructions:

1. **Season steaks:** Rub steaks with olive oil, garlic, parsley, lemon juice, paprika, salt, and pepper.
2. **Grill steaks:** Preheat grill to medium-high heat and grill steaks for 5-6 minutes per side for medium-rare.
3. **Serve:** Let the steaks rest before slicing and serving with chimichurri sauce on the side.

Sesame-Ginger Marinated Steak

Ingredients:

- 2 flank steaks
- 3 tablespoons soy sauce
- 2 tablespoons sesame oil
- 2 tablespoons rice vinegar
- 1 tablespoon fresh ginger, grated
- 1 tablespoon honey
- 2 cloves garlic, minced
- 1 teaspoon chili flakes (optional)

Instructions:

1. **Make marinade:** In a bowl, combine soy sauce, sesame oil, rice vinegar, ginger, honey, garlic, and chili flakes.
2. **Marinate steak:** Coat flank steaks with the marinade and refrigerate for 2 hours.
3. **Grill steaks:** Preheat grill to medium-high heat. Grill steaks for 4-5 minutes per side.
4. **Serve:** Slice thinly against the grain and serve.

Red Chimichurri Picanha

Ingredients:

- 2 picanha steaks
- 1/4 cup red wine vinegar
- 1/4 cup olive oil
- 2 cloves garlic, minced
- 1 tablespoon fresh oregano, chopped
- 1 tablespoon smoked paprika
- 1/4 teaspoon red pepper flakes
- Salt and freshly ground black pepper, to taste

Instructions:

1. **Make chimichurri sauce:** Combine red wine vinegar, olive oil, garlic, oregano, paprika, red pepper flakes, salt, and pepper in a bowl.
2. **Marinate picanha:** Coat the picanha steaks with chimichurri sauce and refrigerate for 1-2 hours.
3. **Grill steaks:** Preheat grill to medium-high heat. Grill steaks for 4-5 minutes per side for medium-rare.
4. **Serve:** Slice the picanha against the grain and serve with the remaining chimichurri sauce.

Grilled Steak Salad with Mustard Vinaigrette

Ingredients:

- 2 sirloin steaks
- Salt and freshly ground black pepper, to taste
- 4 cups mixed salad greens
- 1/2 cup cherry tomatoes, halved
- 1/4 cup red onion, thinly sliced
- 1/4 cup mustard vinaigrette (store-bought or homemade)

Instructions:

1. **Season steaks:** Rub sirloin steaks with salt and pepper.
2. **Grill steaks:** Preheat grill to medium-high heat. Grill steaks for 4-5 minutes per side for medium-rare.
3. **Assemble salad:** Toss salad greens, tomatoes, and onions with mustard vinaigrette.
4. **Serve:** Slice the grilled steaks thinly and arrange on top of the salad. Serve immediately.

Chipotle Lime Flank Steak

Ingredients:

- 2 flank steaks
- 2 tablespoons olive oil
- 1 tablespoon chipotle chili powder
- 1 tablespoon lime juice
- 2 cloves garlic, minced
- Salt and freshly ground black pepper, to taste

Instructions:

1. **Season steaks:** Rub flank steaks with olive oil, chipotle chili powder, lime juice, garlic, salt, and pepper.
2. **Grill steaks:** Preheat grill to medium-high heat and grill steaks for 4-5 minutes per side.
3. **Serve:** Let steaks rest for 5 minutes before slicing thinly and serving.

Steak Fajitas

Ingredients:

- 2 skirt steaks
- 1 tablespoon olive oil
- 1 red bell pepper, sliced
- 1 green bell pepper, sliced
- 1 onion, sliced
- 1 tablespoon lime juice
- 1 teaspoon cumin
- 1 teaspoon chili powder
- Salt and freshly ground black pepper, to taste
- Flour tortillas

Instructions:

1. **Marinate steaks:** Rub skirt steaks with olive oil, lime juice, cumin, chili powder, salt, and pepper. Marinate for 30 minutes.
2. **Cook steak:** Preheat grill or skillet to medium-high heat. Grill steaks for 3-4 minutes per side.
3. **Prepare fajitas:** Sauté bell peppers and onions in a skillet with olive oil until tender.
4. **Serve:** Slice the steak and serve with sautéed peppers, onions, and warm tortillas.

Balsamic Rosemary Hanger Steak

Ingredients:

- 2 hanger steaks
- 1/4 cup balsamic vinegar
- 2 tablespoons olive oil
- 1 tablespoon fresh rosemary, chopped
- 2 cloves garlic, minced
- Salt and freshly ground black pepper, to taste

Instructions:

1. **Make marinade:** Combine balsamic vinegar, olive oil, rosemary, garlic, salt, and pepper in a bowl.
2. **Marinate steak:** Coat hanger steaks with the marinade and refrigerate for 1-2 hours.
3. **Grill steaks:** Preheat grill to medium-high heat. Grill steaks for 4-5 minutes per side for medium-rare.
4. **Serve:** Let steaks rest for 5 minutes before slicing and serving.

Char-Grilled Porterhouse with Compound Butter

Ingredients:

- 2 porterhouse steaks
- Salt and freshly ground black pepper, to taste
- 1/2 cup unsalted butter, softened
- 2 tablespoons fresh parsley, chopped
- 1 tablespoon fresh thyme, chopped
- 1 teaspoon lemon zest

Instructions:

1. **Season steaks:** Season porterhouse steaks with salt and pepper.
2. **Grill steaks:** Preheat grill to high heat. Grill steaks for 5-6 minutes per side.
3. **Make compound butter:** Mix softened butter with parsley, thyme, and lemon zest.
4. **Serve:** Top the steaks with compound butter and serve immediately.

Steak and Mushroom Sauce

Ingredients:

- 2 ribeye steaks
- 2 tablespoons olive oil
- 1 cup mushrooms, sliced
- 2 cloves garlic, minced
- 1/4 cup beef broth
- 1/4 cup heavy cream
- Salt and freshly ground black pepper, to taste

Instructions:

1. **Cook steaks:** Season ribeye steaks with salt and pepper. Sear in olive oil over medium-high heat for 4-5 minutes per side.
2. **Prepare sauce:** In the same pan, sauté mushrooms and garlic until softened. Add beef broth and cream, simmer until thickened.
3. **Serve:** Serve the steaks with the mushroom sauce on top.

Citrus-Marinated Tri-Tip

Ingredients:

- 1 tri-tip steak
- 1/4 cup orange juice
- 2 tablespoons lime juice
- 2 tablespoons olive oil
- 2 cloves garlic, minced
- 1 teaspoon ground cumin
- Salt and freshly ground black pepper, to taste

Instructions:

1. **Make marinade:** Combine orange juice, lime juice, olive oil, garlic, cumin, salt, and pepper in a bowl.
2. **Marinate tri-tip:** Coat tri-tip with the marinade and refrigerate for 2 hours.
3. **Grill steak:** Preheat grill to medium-high heat. Grill tri-tip for 5-6 minutes per side for medium-rare.
4. **Serve:** Slice the tri-tip against the grain and serve.

Garlic Butter Steak Bites

Ingredients:

- 1 lb sirloin steak, cut into bite-sized pieces
- 3 tablespoons butter
- 3 cloves garlic, minced
- 1 tablespoon fresh parsley, chopped
- Salt and freshly ground black pepper, to taste
- 1 teaspoon paprika

Instructions:

1. **Season steak bites:** Season the steak pieces with salt, pepper, and paprika.
2. **Cook steak:** In a skillet, melt butter over medium-high heat. Add steak bites and sear for 2-3 minutes per side until browned and cooked through.
3. **Garlic butter:** Add minced garlic to the pan and cook for 1 minute.
4. **Serve:** Toss the steak bites in the garlic butter and sprinkle with fresh parsley before serving.

Steak Skewers with Peanut Sauce

Ingredients:

- 1 lb flank steak, cut into 1-inch cubes
- 1 tablespoon olive oil
- Salt and freshly ground black pepper, to taste
- 1/2 cup peanut butter
- 1 tablespoon soy sauce
- 1 tablespoon lime juice
- 1 tablespoon honey
- 1 teaspoon ginger, grated
- 2 tablespoons water

Instructions:

1. **Prepare steak skewers:** Thread steak cubes onto skewers, brush with olive oil, and season with salt and pepper.
2. **Grill steak:** Preheat grill to medium-high heat. Grill the skewers for 3-4 minutes per side, until desired doneness.
3. **Make peanut sauce:** In a small bowl, whisk together peanut butter, soy sauce, lime juice, honey, ginger, and water.
4. **Serve:** Drizzle the peanut sauce over the steak skewers and serve.

Cajun Steak Alfredo

Ingredients:

- 2 ribeye steaks
- 1 tablespoon Cajun seasoning
- 2 tablespoons olive oil
- 2 cloves garlic, minced
- 1 cup heavy cream
- 1/2 cup Parmesan cheese, grated
- 8 oz fettuccine pasta, cooked
- Salt and freshly ground black pepper, to taste

Instructions:

1. **Season steaks:** Rub ribeye steaks with Cajun seasoning.
2. **Cook steaks:** Heat olive oil in a skillet over medium-high heat. Sear steaks for 4-5 minutes per side for medium-rare. Let rest before slicing.
3. **Make Alfredo sauce:** In the same skillet, add minced garlic and cook for 1 minute. Add heavy cream and bring to a simmer. Stir in Parmesan and cook until the sauce thickens.
4. **Serve:** Toss cooked pasta in the Alfredo sauce. Top with sliced steak and serve.

Spicy Thai Basil Beef

Ingredients:

- 1 lb ground beef
- 2 tablespoons vegetable oil
- 3 cloves garlic, minced
- 1 red chili, sliced
- 2 tablespoons soy sauce
- 1 tablespoon fish sauce
- 1 tablespoon sugar
- 1/4 cup fresh basil leaves, chopped

Instructions:

1. **Cook beef:** Heat oil in a skillet over medium-high heat. Add ground beef and cook until browned.
2. **Make sauce:** Add garlic, chili, soy sauce, fish sauce, and sugar to the beef. Cook for 2 minutes.
3. **Add basil:** Stir in fresh basil leaves and cook for another minute.
4. **Serve:** Serve the spicy Thai basil beef with steamed rice.

Steak and Shrimp Surf & Turf

Ingredients:

- 2 filet mignon steaks
- 8 large shrimp, peeled and deveined
- 2 tablespoons butter
- 2 cloves garlic, minced
- 1 tablespoon lemon juice
- Salt and freshly ground black pepper, to taste
- 1 tablespoon fresh parsley, chopped

Instructions:

1. **Cook steaks:** Season filet mignon steaks with salt and pepper. Sear in a skillet over medium-high heat for 4-5 minutes per side. Let rest.
2. **Cook shrimp:** In the same skillet, melt butter and add garlic. Cook shrimp for 2-3 minutes per side, until pink.
3. **Finish:** Add lemon juice to the skillet and stir to combine.
4. **Serve:** Plate the steaks and top with shrimp. Garnish with fresh parsley and serve.

Maple Glazed Steak Tips

Ingredients:

- 1 lb steak tips (any tender cut)
- 2 tablespoons olive oil
- 1/4 cup maple syrup
- 2 tablespoons soy sauce
- 2 cloves garlic, minced
- 1 tablespoon Dijon mustard
- Salt and freshly ground black pepper, to taste

Instructions:

1. **Season steak tips:** Season steak tips with salt and pepper.
2. **Cook steak tips:** Heat olive oil in a skillet over medium-high heat. Cook steak tips for 3-4 minutes per side until browned and cooked to your liking.
3. **Make maple glaze:** In a bowl, whisk together maple syrup, soy sauce, garlic, and Dijon mustard. Pour over the steak tips in the skillet.
4. **Serve:** Cook for an additional minute to thicken the glaze, then serve the steak tips with the maple sauce.

Sous Vide Filet Mignon

Ingredients:

- 2 filet mignon steaks
- Salt and freshly ground black pepper, to taste
- 2 tablespoons butter
- 1 sprig rosemary
- 2 cloves garlic, crushed

Instructions:

1. **Season steaks:** Season filet mignon steaks with salt and pepper.
2. **Sous vide:** Seal steaks in a vacuum bag and cook sous vide at 130°F (54°C) for 1-2 hours.
3. **Sear steaks:** After cooking, heat a skillet over high heat and sear the steaks for 1-2 minutes per side with butter, rosemary, and garlic.
4. **Serve:** Let rest for 5 minutes before serving.

Grilled Steak with Blackberry Sauce

Ingredients:

- 2 ribeye steaks
- Salt and freshly ground black pepper, to taste
- 1/2 cup blackberries
- 2 tablespoons balsamic vinegar
- 1 tablespoon honey
- 1 teaspoon fresh thyme, chopped

Instructions:

1. **Season steaks:** Season ribeye steaks with salt and pepper.
2. **Grill steaks:** Preheat grill to medium-high heat. Grill steaks for 4-5 minutes per side.
3. **Make blackberry sauce:** In a saucepan, combine blackberries, balsamic vinegar, honey, and thyme. Simmer for 5 minutes until the sauce thickens.
4. **Serve:** Spoon the blackberry sauce over the steaks and serve.

Herb-Crusted Prime Ribeye

Ingredients:

- 2 prime ribeye steaks
- 2 tablespoons olive oil
- 2 cloves garlic, minced
- 1 tablespoon fresh rosemary, chopped
- 1 tablespoon fresh thyme, chopped
- Salt and freshly ground black pepper, to taste

Instructions:

1. **Prepare steaks:** Rub ribeye steaks with olive oil, garlic, rosemary, thyme, salt, and pepper.
2. **Cook steaks:** Heat a skillet over medium-high heat and cook the steaks for 4-5 minutes per side until medium-rare.
3. **Serve:** Let the steaks rest for 5 minutes before serving.

Braised Short Ribs with Red Wine Reduction

Ingredients:

- 4 beef short ribs
- Salt and freshly ground black pepper, to taste
- 2 tablespoons olive oil
- 2 onions, chopped
- 3 cloves garlic, minced
- 2 cups red wine
- 1 cup beef broth
- 2 sprigs fresh rosemary
- 1 sprig fresh thyme

Instructions:

1. **Brown short ribs:** Season short ribs with salt and pepper. Heat olive oil in a large pot over medium-high heat. Brown ribs on all sides for 5-6 minutes.
2. **Prepare braise:** Add onions and garlic, cook for 3 minutes. Add red wine, beef broth, rosemary, and thyme. Bring to a simmer.
3. **Braise:** Cover and cook in the oven at 350°F (175°C) for 2-3 hours until tender.
4. **Finish sauce:** Remove short ribs and strain the sauce. Simmer sauce until it thickens, then serve over the short ribs.

www.ingramcontent.com/pod-product-compliance
Lightning Source LLC
LaVergne TN
LVHW081335060526
838201LV00055B/2668